BY ASHLEY GISH

NATIONAL WOMEN'S SOCCER LEAGUE

BELLWETHER MEDIA • MINNEAPOLIS, MN

Torque brims with excitement perfect for thrill-seekers of all kinds. Discover daring survival skills, explore uncharted worlds, and marvel at mighty engines and extreme sports. In *Torque* books, anything can happen. Are you ready?

This edition first published in 2025 by Bellwether Media, Inc.

No part of this publication may be reproduced in whole or in part without written permission of the publisher. For information regarding permission, write to Bellwether Media, Inc., Attention: Permissions Department, 6012 Blue Circle Drive, Minnetonka, MN 55343.

Library of Congress Cataloging-in-Publication Data

Names: Gish, Ashley, author.
Title: National women's soccer league / by Ashley Gish.
Description: Minneapolis, MN : Bellwether Media, Inc., 2025. | Series: Torque: Soccer leagues | Includes bibliographical references and index. | Audience: Ages 7-12 | Audience: Grades 4-6 | Summary: "Engaging images accompany information about the National Women's Soccer League. The combination of high-interest subject matter and light text is intended for students in grades 3 through 7" – Provided by publisher.
Identifiers: LCCN 2024022703 (print) | LCCN 2024022704 (ebook) | ISBN 9798893040258 (library binding) | ISBN 9781644879610 (ebook)
Subjects: LCSH: Soccer for women–Juvenile literature. | National Women's Soccer League–Juvenile literature. | Women soccer players–Juvenile literature. | Soccer–History–Juvenile literature.
Classification: LCC GV944.5 .G58 2025 (print) | LCC GV944.5 (ebook) | DDC 796.334/62082–dc23/eng/20240524
LC record available at https://lccn.loc.gov/2024022703
LC ebook record available at https://lccn.loc.gov/2024022704
Library of Congress Cataloging-in-Publication Data

Text copyright © 2025 by Bellwether Media, Inc. TORQUE and associated logos are trademarks and/or registered trademarks of Bellwether Media, Inc. Bellwether Media is a division of Chrysalis Education Group.

Editor: Kieran Downs   Designer: Gabriel Hilger

Printed in the United States of America, North Mankato, MN.

TABLE OF CONTENTS

AN EXCITING MATCH	4
WHAT IS THE NATIONAL WOMEN'S SOCCER LEAGUE?	6
HISTORY OF THE NATIONAL WOMEN'S SOCCER LEAGUE	8
THE NATIONAL WOMEN'S SOCCER LEAGUE TODAY	12
FAST FACTS	20
GLOSSARY	22
TO LEARN MORE	23
INDEX	24

AN EXCITING MATCH

It is the 2021 National Women's Soccer League (NWSL) **Championship** match. The Washington Spirit are up against the Chicago Red Stars. The match is in **extra time**.

In the 97th minute of the match, the Spirit move the ball near the net. They take the shot. **Goal**! The crowd cheers as the Spirit win the match. They are champions of the 2021 season!

WASHINGTON SPIRIT

WHAT IS THE NATIONAL WOMEN'S SOCCER LEAGUE?

The National Women's Soccer League is the top women's soccer league in the United States. It attracts great players from all over the world.

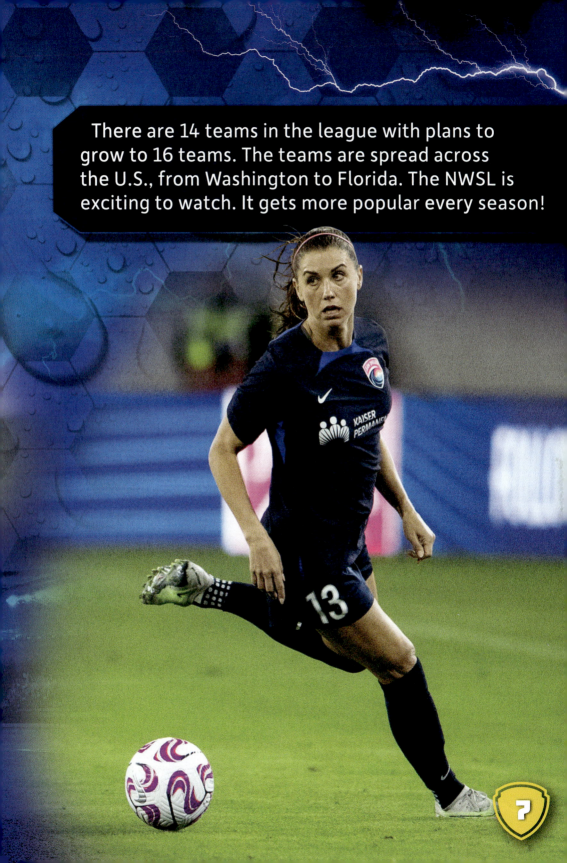

There are 14 teams in the league with plans to grow to 16 teams. The teams are spread across the U.S., from Washington to Florida. The NWSL is exciting to watch. It gets more popular every season!

HISTORY OF THE NATIONAL WOMEN'S SOCCER LEAGUE

The first U.S. **professional** women's soccer league came together in 2001. It was called the Women's United Soccer Association. But few fans watched matches. The league soon broke apart.

A new top league called Women's Professional Soccer took over in 2009. Its last season ended in 2012. That year, officials met to make a new league. The NWSL was formed.

TIMELINE

2001
The Women's United Soccer Association begins play

2003
The Women's United Soccer Association plays its last season

2009
Women's Professional Soccer begins play

2003 WOMEN'S UNITED SOCCER ASSOCIATION MATCH

GAME ON

The Portland Thorns and FC Kansas City played the first NWSL match on April 13, 2013. It ended in a tie.

2013
The NWSL begins its first season

2024
The league grows to 14 teams

In 2013, NWSL matches began. Eight teams played in the league. The Portland Thorns won the first championship.

The league grew quickly over the years. Many star players joined the league, including many from the U.S. Women's National Team. This brought in new fans. In 2024, the league grew to 14 teams. Two more teams plan to join in 2026.

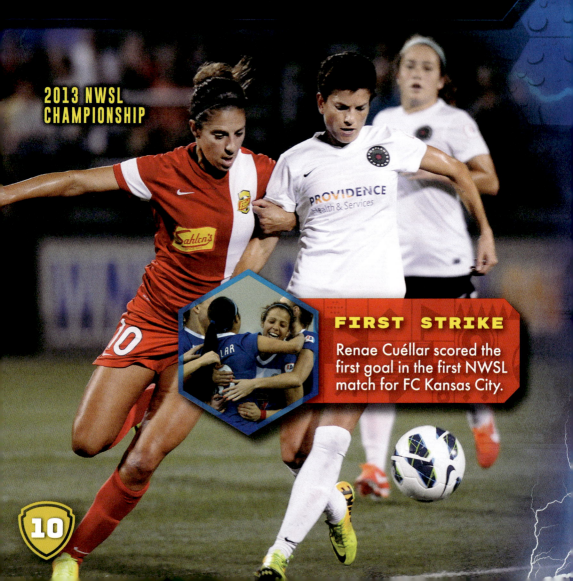

2013 NWSL CHAMPIONSHIP

FIRST STRIKE
Renae Cuéllar scored the first goal in the first NWSL match for FC Kansas City.

FOUNDING TEAMS

- Boston Breakers
- Chicago Red Stars
- FC Kansas City
- Portland Thorns FC
- Seattle Reign FC
- Sky Blue FC
- Washington Spirit
- Western New York Flash

THE NATIONAL WOMEN'S SOCCER LEAGUE TODAY

The National Women's Soccer League begins in March with the **Challenge Cup**. The top regular season team from the previous season plays against the team that won the NWSL Championship.

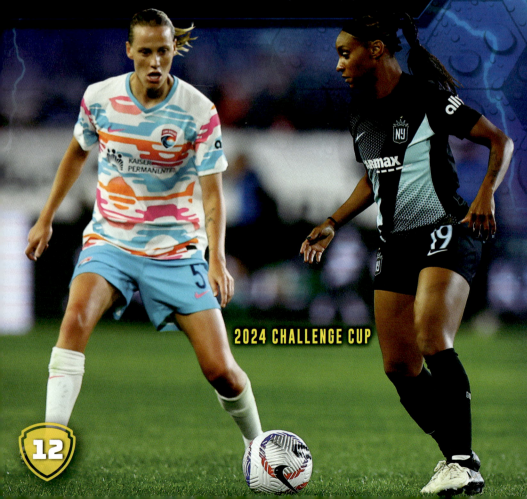

2024 CHALLENGE CUP

The regular season also begins in March. Each team plays each other twice. The NWSL takes a break in July. The regular season ends in early November.

NWSL teams are ranked based on how well they play. Teams earn three points for a win. They earn one point for a tie. They earn zero points for a loss.

14

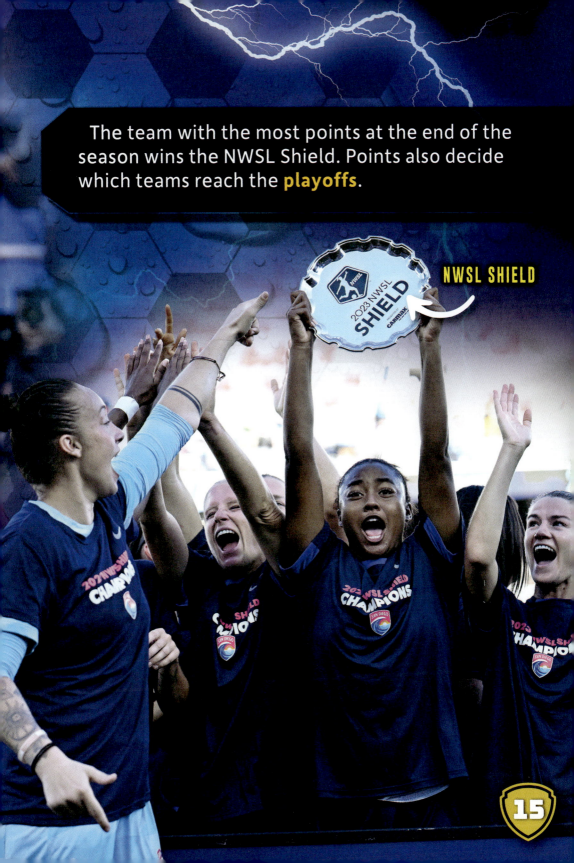

The team with the most points at the end of the season wins the NWSL Shield. Points also decide which teams reach the **playoffs**.

NWSL SHIELD

The eight teams with the most points at the end of the season reach the playoffs. Teams are **seeded** based on points. Teams with higher points play against teams with lower points first.

Teams play against each other in this **tournament** until only one team is left. That team gets the NWSL Championship trophy!

2023 NWSL PLAYOFFS

NWSL PLAYOFFS

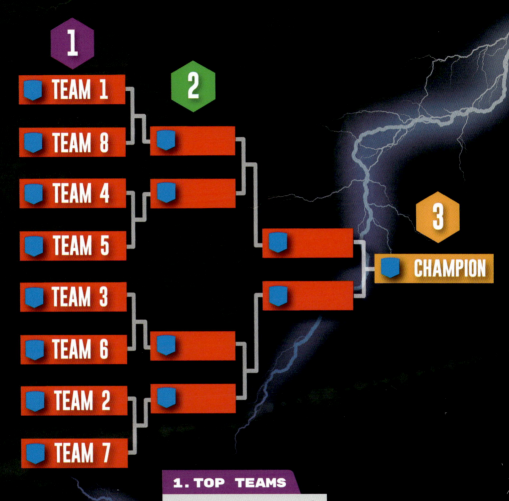

1. TOP TEAMS
The top 8 teams reach the playoffs.

2. ELIMINATION
Teams play elimination matches.

3. CHAMPIONSHIP
The last team standing wins the championship.

NWSL matches have gained popularity over the years. More and more fans go to matches. New teams also attract new fans.

NWSL Fan Fest is a fun way for fans to support their favorite teams. They can get **autographs**, make signs, and have their faces painted. Fans love to cheer for their favorite NWSL teams!

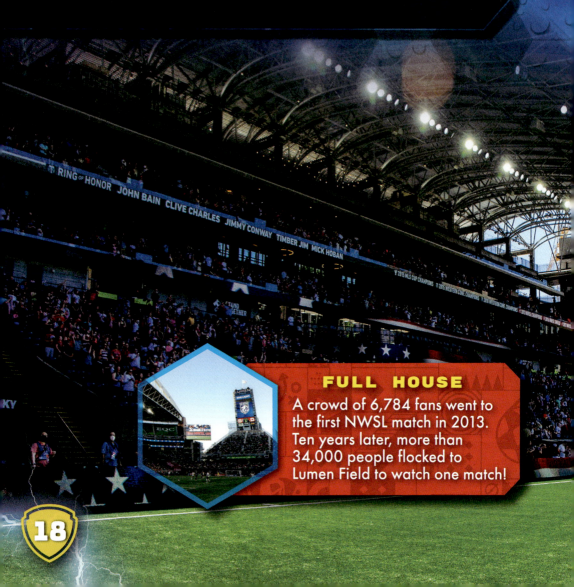

FULL HOUSE
A crowd of 6,784 fans went to the first NWSL match in 2013. Ten years later, more than 34,000 people flocked to Lumen Field to watch one match!

TOP PLAYERS

MEGAN RAPINOE

15 — FORWARD
Played for Seattle Reign FC, 2013–2023

CHRISTINE SINCLAIR

12 — FORWARD
Played for Portland Thorns FC, 2013–2024

LYNN WILLIAMS

10 — FORWARD
Played for NJ/NY Gotham FC, 2023–present

ALEX MORGAN

13 — FORWARD
Played for San Diego Wave FC, 2022–present

SOPHIA SMITH

9 — FORWARD
Played for Portland Thorns FC, 2021–present

FAST FACTS

NUMBER OF TEAMS	14
YEAR STARTED	2013

LARGEST STADIUM

SNAPDRAGON STADIUM
SAN DIEGO WAVE

Capacity: 35,000 people
Location: San Diego, California

CLUB RECORDS
(AS OF 2023)

CLUBS WITH MOST APPEARANCES
CHICAGO RED STARS, NJ/NY GOTHAM FC, SEATTLE REIGN FC, PORTLAND THORNS FC, WASHINGTON SPIRIT
11 SEASONS

CLUB WITH MOST CHAMPIONSHIPS
PORTLAND THORNS FC
3

FIRST CHAMPION
PORTLAND THORNS FC

CLUBS THAT HAVE PARTICIPATED IN THE LEAGUE
16

INDIVIDUAL RECORDS
(AS OF 2023)

Most career league goals
Sam Kerr: 78 goals

Most goals scored in a single season
Sam Kerr: 18 Goals

Fastest goal scored
Michelle Cooper: 22 seconds

Person with most league appearances
Lauren Barnes: 211 Appearances

GLOSSARY

autographs—the names of famous people that are written by them

Challenge Cup—a match between the winner of the NWSL Championship and the team with the best regular season record

championship—a contest to decide the best team or person

extra time—time added to the end of soccer matches to make up for stoppage time

goal—a score in soccer; a player scores a goal by sending the ball into the other team's net.

playoffs—matches played after the regular season is over; playoff matches determine which teams play in the championship match.

professional—related to a player or team that makes money playing a sport

seeded—ranked based on results to help a team go further in a tournament

tournament—a series of matches in which several teams try to win the championship

TO LEARN MORE

AT THE LIBRARY

Golkar, Golriz. *Alex Morgan*. Minneapolis, Minn.: Bellwether Media, 2024.

Golkar, Golriz. *Megan Rapinoe*. Minneapolis, Minn.: Bellwether Media, 2024.

McDougall, Chrös. *Soccer*. Minneapolis, Minn: ABDO, 2024.

ON THE WEB

FACTSURFER

Factsurfer.com gives you a safe, fun way to find more information.

1. Go to www.factsurfer.com

2. Enter "National Women's Soccer League" into the search box and click 🔍.

3. Select your book cover to see a list of related content.

INDEX

Challenge Cup, 12
Cuéllar, Renae, 10
extra time, 4
fans, 8, 10, 18
fast facts, 20–21
founding teams, 11
goal, 4, 10
history, 4, 8, 9, 10, 11, 18
match, 4, 8, 9, 10, 18
NWSL Championship, 4, 10, 12, 16
NWSL Fan Fest, 18
NWSL Shield, 15
players, 6, 10, 19
playoffs, 15, 16, 17
points, 14, 15, 16
season, 4, 7, 12, 13, 15, 16
seeded, 16
teams, 4, 7, 9, 10, 11, 12, 13, 14, 15, 16, 18
timeline, 8–9
top players, 19
United States, 6, 7
U.S. Women's National Team, 10
Women's Professional Soccer, 8
Women's United Soccer Association, 8, 9

The images in this book are reproduced through the courtesy of: Nick Tre. Smith/ Icon Sportswire/ AP Images, cover; Findlay/ Alamy, p. 3; Jeff Dean/ AP Images, pp. 4, 5; Amanda Loman/ AP Images, p. 6; SPP Sport Press Photo./ Alamy, pp. 7, 18, 21 (Michelle Cooper); Women's Professional Soccer/ Wiki Commons, p. 8 (2001); LENNY IGNELZI/ AP Images, p. 8 (2003); Women's United Soccer Association/ Wiki Commons, p. 8 (2007); JOHN BAZEMORE/ AP Images, p. 9 (2003 Women's United Soccer Association match); Brian Davidson/ AP Images, pp. 9 (Game On), 10 (First Strike); National Women's Soccer League/ Wiki Commons, pp. 9 (2013), 11 (NWSL Team Logos), 20 (NWSL Logo); ZUMA Press, Inc./ Alamy, pp. 9 (2024), 19 (Megan Rapinoe), 20, 21 (Lauren Barnes); Alan Schwartz/ AP Images, p. 10 (2013 NWSL Championship); Rich Graessle/ Icon Sportswire/ AP Images, p. 12; Cal Sport Media/ Alamy, pp. 13, 15, 19 (Christine Sinclair, Alex Morgan); Thurman James/ AP Images, p. 14; Lindsey Wasson/ AP Images, pp. 16, 18 (Full House); Rebekah Wynkoop/ SPP/ AP Images, p. 19 (Lynn Williams); Al Sermeno/ Alamy, p. 19 (Sophia Smith); Kirby Lee/ Alamy, p. 20 (Snapdragon Stadium); Robin Alam/ Icon Sportswire/ AP Images, p. 21 (Sam Kerr); Brazil Photo Press/ Alamy, p. 23.